Cat-ographies

Abyssinians
Egyptian Royalty?

by Dawn Bluemel Oldfield

Consultant: Norman Auspitz
The Cat Fanciers' Association Abyssinian Breed Council Secretary

BEARPORT
PUBLISHING

New York, New York

Credits

Cover and Title Page, © Alan Robinson/Animal Photography; TOC, © Utekhina Anna/Shutterstock; 4T, © Sally Anne Thompson/Animal Photography; 4B, © Chris Hill/Scenic Ireland; 5, © Peter Hasselbom; 6T, © Roger Wood/Corbis; 6B, © Glow Images/SuperStock; 7L, © Statuette of the goddess Bastet, Third Intermediate Period (bronze) by Egyptian 25th Dynasty (780-656 BC) Louvre, Paris, France/Giraudon/The Bridgeman Art Library; 7R, © Karen McGougan/BCIUSA/Photoshot; 9, © Mary Evans Picture Library; 10, © Helmi Flick/Animal Photography; 11, © Tomasz Wojtasik/EPA/Landov; 12, © Helmi Flick/Animal Photography; 13L, © Helmi Flick/Animal Photography; 13TR, © Helmi Flick/Animal Photography; 13MR, © R. Richter/Tierfotoagentur/Alamy; 13BR, © Tetsu Yamazaki/Animal Photography; 14, © Peter Hasselbom; 15T, © Oleg Alexeev/AbySphere Cattery/www.abyssincat.ru; 15B, © Peter Hasselbom; 16T, © Tetsu Yamazaki/Animal Photography; 16B, © Sally Anne Thompson/Animal Photography; 17, © Peter Hasselbom; 18, © AP Images/L.G. Patterson; 19, © Corbis/SuperStock; 20L, © Anobis/Shutterstock; 20R, © Christina Gandolfo/Flickr/Getty Images; 21, © Corbis/SuperStock; 22, © Richard Katris/Chanan Photography; 23, © Aivolie/Shutterstock.

Publisher: Kenn Goin
Editorial Director: Adam Siegel
Creative Director: Spencer Brinker
Design: Dawn Beard Creative
Photo Researcher: Omni-Photo Communications, Inc.

Library of Congress Cataloging-in-Publication Data

Bluemel Oldfield, Dawn.
  Abyssinians : Egyptian royalty? / by Dawn Bluemel Oldfield.
     p. cm. — (Cat-ographies)
  Includes bibliographical references and index.
  ISBN-13: 978-1-61772-145-8 (library binding)
  ISBN-10: 1-61772-145-X (library binding)
  1. Abyssinian cat—Juvenile literature. I. Title.
  SF449.A28B58 2011
  636.8'26—dc22
                      2010038751

For more information, write to Bearport Publishing Company, Inc., 101 Fifth Avenue, Suite 6R, New York, New York 10003. Printed in the United States of America in North Mankato, Minnesota.

122010
10810CGD

10 9 8 7 6 5 4 3 2 1

Contents

Cats of the Castle 4

An Egyptian Cat? 6

Out of Africa 8

Winning Looks 10

Fancy Fur 12

Clowns of the Cat World 14

Aby Babies 16

Caring for Abyssinians 18

Playful Pets 20

Abyssinians at a Glance 22

Glossary 23

Index 24

Bibliography 24

Read More 24

Learn More Online 24

About the Author 24

Cats of the Castle

It is early morning at Springfield Castle in Ireland. Tanzania, an Abyssinian (*ab*-uh-SIN-ee-uhn) cat, creeps quietly across the ground. She is teaching her kittens, FatCat and Sphinx (SFINKS), how to hunt. It is their job to stop mice and other **rodents** from eating vegetables in the gardens and fields around the castle.

An Abyssinian's muscular body is designed for hunting.

Springfield Castle in Drumcollogher, Ireland

People first brought cats to England from other parts of Europe about 2,000 years ago. The cats were used to keep mice and rats out of buildings where grain was stored. It wasn't long before the cats made their home in nearby Ireland as well.

Sphinx, tail and whiskers twitching, sees something move in a row of corn. The tiny Abyssinian leaps into the air and pounces on a gray mouse. Sphinx picks up the animal with his sharp teeth, purring with pride. He has learned his lesson well.

Abyssinians can run up to 30 miles per hour (48 kph) and can jump more than six feet (1.8 m) into the air.

An Egyptian Cat?

Sphinx lives in Ireland, but he was named after a statue that was built in ancient Egypt. Why? Some people think Abyssinian cats were first raised in Egypt thousands of years ago. They believe this because Abyssinians look like the cats in ancient Egyptian art and **hieroglyphics**.

This sculpture of a cat was made more than 2,000 years ago in Egypt.

The Sphinx is a famous statue that was built about 4,500 years ago in Egypt. It has the head of a man and the body of a lion.

Honored for their hunting skills, the cats of ancient Egypt protected the country's grain from mice. The people of Egypt didn't just admire the cats because they were good hunters, however. They believed the cats were **sacred**. They thought the furry animals were closely connected to one of their gods—Bastet. As a result, people **worshipped** the cats—and the punishment for killing one was death.

Bastet was often shown as having the body of a woman and the head of a cat.

Egyptians believed Bastet had glowing eyes that could magically see in the dark. Since cats' eyes appear to glow at night, people thought the animals had great powers.

Out of Africa

No one knows for sure if Abyssinian cats came from ancient Egypt. Some people think the cats first roamed the jungles of Abyssinia, a kingdom in eastern Africa that covered what is now called Ethiopia and Eritrea. The wild animals were tamed there thousands of years ago and became popular pets. How did these cats find their way to other parts of the world?

Where Abyssinian Cats Came From

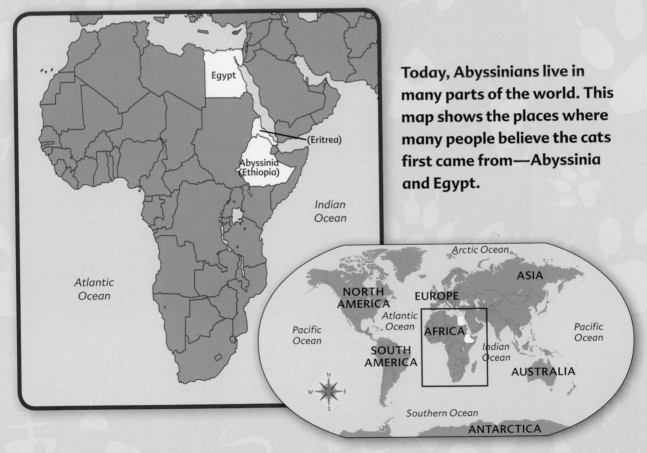

Today, Abyssinians live in many parts of the world. This map shows the places where many people believe the cats first came from—Abyssinia and Egypt.

In 1868, Great Britain was at war with Abyssinia. After the fighting ended, the British Navy was ready to sail home. Before one of the British captains returned to England, however, a little Abyssinian kitten caught his attention. He brought the kitten home and named her Zula. The little cat was probably the first Abyssinian cat, or Aby, in England.

A drawing of Zula

The first Abyssinian cats arrived in the United States in the early 1900s. Their names were Aluminum II and Salt.

Winning Looks

People in England fell in love with Zula's beautiful and unusual appearance. The cat's wedge-shaped face looked like an upside-down triangle. She had large ears and almond-shaped eyes. Her shiny **coat** made up of light and dark hair gave her a striking look. It wasn't long before other Abyssinians were brought to England as well.

An Aby's eyes are usually golden, but they can also be green or **hazel**.

In 1871, a cat owner entered an Abyssinian in a cat show in London. The cat competed against other **breeds** such as Siamese and Persians. The Aby won third place! Judges were impressed with her beautiful looks and playful personality.

Abyssinians are still popular at cat shows today.

Fancy Fur

Whichever country Abyssinians came from, they are now admired for their beauty all over the world. Because of their long, lean legs, Abyssinians are called the "runway models" of cat shows. They dramatically pose for judges, flicking their long tails.

An Aby's small paws and long legs often make it look like the cat is standing on tiptoe.

What else makes these cats look so unique? It is their **ticked** fur. Each hair on an Aby's coat has four or more bands of color that is light at the base and dark at the tip. Most Abyssinians are ruddy-colored (orange-brown). However, some are red (red-copper), blue (blue-gray), or fawn (pale cream).

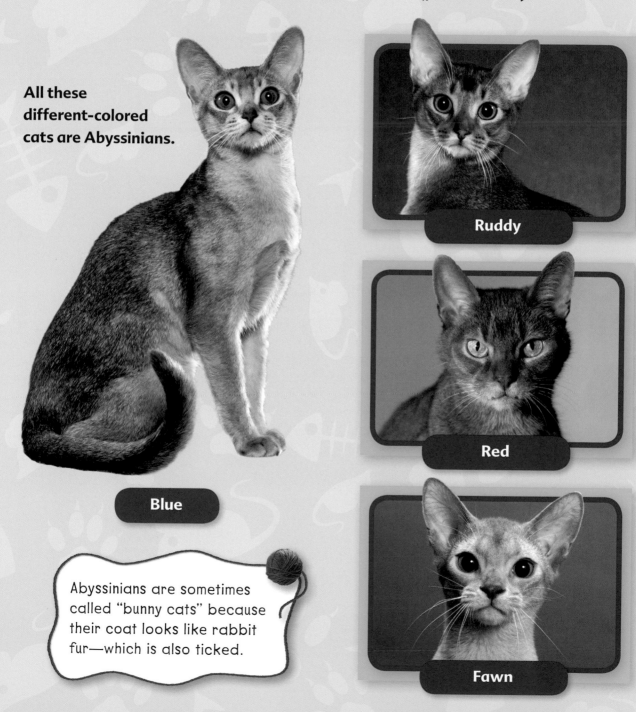

All these different-colored cats are Abyssinians.

Ruddy

Red

Blue

Fawn

Abyssinians are sometimes called "bunny cats" because their coat looks like rabbit fur—which is also ticked.

Clowns of the Cat World

The Abyssinian is nicknamed the clown of cats. Nothing is off limits for these **mischievous** animals. They like pushing objects off shelves or cabinets. They are also clever and can open drawers and cupboards.

If owners don't lock their drawers, an Aby might open them to find out what is inside.

Abyssinians are curious creatures that like to watch what their owners are doing. Sometimes they want to get involved as well. An Abyssinian may "help" its owner type by tiptoeing across a keyboard. People who are preparing food may find their Abys curled up in a bowl.

Most cats hate water—but not Abyssinians. They like to play with water and think it is fun to dip their paw under a running faucet. They even like to swim!

This Aby wants to help its owner make dinner.

Aby Babies

Abyssinian females have a **litter** of two to four kittens. Small and helpless, each tiny Aby weighs about four ounces (113 g) when it is born—less than the weight of a baseball. Newborn kittens can't see because their eyes are closed. They won't open for about two weeks.

Like all cats, Aby kittens are born with blue eyes. Their eyes change color by the time they are a few months old.

Kittens that can't see yet use touch and smell to help them find their mother and her milk.

When they are first born, kittens get all the food they need by drinking their mother's milk. By the time they are about six weeks old, they begin to eat kitten food.

Week by week the kittens grow bigger and stronger. They begin to crawl and explore their world. Soon they become more daring, pouncing and wrestling with one another. They purr loudly to get attention. After 12 weeks the cute, friendly kittens are strong enough to leave their mother and become part of a human family.

Play fighting isn't just fun for kittens. It helps them try out the skills they will need when hunting.

Caring for Abyssinians

Abyssinians are usually healthy cats. However, they still need to go to a **veterinarian** for yearly checkups. Like people, they need **vaccinations** to keep them from getting diseases. Owners should also brush their cats' teeth at least once a week. This will help prevent them from getting gum disease.

This Abyssinian is going to have its teeth checked during its visit to the veterinarian.

Abyssinians clean their fur and skin with their rough tongues. However, it is also important for owners to **groom** their Abys once a week. Gentle brushing removes loose hairs and dirt—and Abys love the attention! They enjoy being stroked and brushed by their owners.

An Abyssinian grooming its paw

Like all cats, Abyssinians spend two to three hours a day licking and cleaning themselves.

Playful Pets

Abyssinians are small animals with big **personalities**! Although Abys are **affectionate**, they would rather play with their owners than cuddle up in their laps. In some ways, the cats are a bit like dogs. Abys learn games and tricks quickly. Some of them even like to play **fetch**.

Abyssinians use their small, bell-like voices to communicate.

Abyssinians get along well with children and other cats—as well as dogs.

Owning an Aby is a big responsibility. People must be willing to give the cats plenty of toys and attention to keep them from getting bored. As long as they do this, owners will find out that a happy, entertained Abyssinian is the "purr-fect" family pet!

Abyssinians at a Glance

Weight:	About 7–12 pounds (3–5 kg)
Height at Shoulder:	10–14 inches (25–36 cm)
Colors:	Ruddy (orange-brown), red (red-copper), blue (blue-gray), or fawn (pale cream)
Country of Origin:	Egypt or Abyssinia
Coat Hair:	Ticked fur that has four or more bands of color; it is light at the base and dark at the tip
Life Span:	9–15 years, sometimes longer
Personality:	Playful, intelligent, curious, athletic; like to be with people; usually get along well with other cats and dogs
Special Physical Characteristics:	Long, lean legs; small, oval-shaped paws; large ears; wedge-shaped face; almond-shaped eyes; ticked fur

Glossary

affectionate (uh-FEK-shuh-nuht) loving

breeds (BREEDZ) types or certain kinds of animals

coat (KOHT) the fur on a cat or other animal

fetch (FECH) to chase after something and then bring it back

groom (GROOM) to brush and clean an animal

hazel (HAY-zuhl) greenish-brown

hieroglyphics (*hye*-ur-uh-GLIF-iks) writings used by ancient Egyptians, made up of pictures and symbols

litter (LIT-ur) a group of baby animals, such as kittens or puppies, that are born to the same mother at the same time.

mischievous (MISS-chuh-vuhss) able to cause trouble, often through playful behavior

personalities (*pur*-suh-NAL-uh-teez) special habits and ways of behaving that make a person or animal different from others

rodents (ROH-duhnts) small mammals with long front teeth, such as mice, rats, squirrels, and beavers

sacred (SAY-krid) holy, religious

ticked (TIKT) having hair that has bands of colors

vaccinations (*vak*-suh-NAY-shuhnz) medicines that protect people and pets against diseases

veterinarian (*vet*-ur-uh-NER-ee-uhn) a doctor who cares for animals

worshipped (WUR-shipt) showed love and devotion to something or someone

Index

Abyssinia 8–9, 22

Bastet 7

care 18–19, 21

coat 10, 13, 22

colors 13, 16, 22

Egypt 6–7, 8, 22

England 4, 9, 10

Ethiopia 8

eyes 7, 10, 16, 22

food 16

grooming 19

height 22

Ireland 4, 6

kittens 4, 9, 16–17

life span 22

personality 11, 14–15, 20, 22

Sphinx 4–5, 6

ticked fur 13, 22

United States 9

veterinarian 18

weight 16, 22

Zula 9, 10

Bibliography

Helgren, J. Anne. *Barron's Encyclopedia of Cat Breeds: A Complete Guide to the Domestic Cats of North America.* Hauppauge, NY: Barron's (1997).

Surman, Richard. *Castle Cats of Britain and Ireland.* London: HarperCollins (1995).

Track, Judah. *Guide to Owning an Abyssinan Cat.* Neptune City, NJ: T.F.H. Publications (1997).

Read More

Hanson, Anders. *Awesome Abyssinians.* Edina, MN: ABDO (2010).

Stone, Lynn M. *Abyssinian Cats.* Vero Beach, FL: Rourke (2010).

Learn More Online

To learn more about Abyssinian cats, visit
www.bearportpublishing.com/Cat-ographies

About the Author

Dawn Bluemel Oldfield is a freelance writer. Crazy about cats, she lives in Prosper, Texas, with her husband and their two fabulous felines, a Siamese mix named Victoria and a tabby named Stella.